Astronaut

poems by

Brian Henry

Carnegie Mellon University Press
Pittsburgh 2002

Acknowledgments

The author is grateful to the editors of the following publications, in which these poems, sometimes in different forms, have appeared: *The Age* (Australia), *American Letters & Commentary*, *American Poetry: The Next Generation* (Carnegie Mellon University Press), *American Poetry Review*, *Arena Magazine* (Australia), *Barrow Street*, *Black Warrior Review*, *The Boston Phoenix*, *Boston Review*, *College Green* (Ireland), *Colorado Review*, *Cordite* (Australia), *CrossRoads: A Journal of Southern Culture*, *Famous Reporter* (Australia), *Force 10* (Ireland), *Hanging Loose*, *The Iowa Review*, *Island* (Australia), *Kunapipi* (UK), *The Massachusetts Review*, *Metre* (Ireland), *Michigan Quarterly Review*, *New American Writing*, *The New Criterion*, *New England Review*, *Overland* (Australia), *The Paris Review*, *Pisi mi Medana* (Slovenia), *Plastic* (Czech Republic), *Poetry Ireland Review*, *Poetry Wales*, *The Prose Poem: An International Journal*, *Salt* (Australia), *Slope* (www.slope.org), *Soundings: Poetry and Poetics* (Australia), *Southern Humanities Review*, *Southern Poetry Review*, *Stand* (UK), *TriQuarterly*, *Ulitarra* (Australia), *Volt*, *Westerly* (Australia), *The William and Mary Review*, and *The Yale Review*.

For personal and editorial support during the writing of these poems, gratitude and thanks go to Henry Hart, Kevin Hart, Glyn Maxwell, Tara Rebele, Peter Richards, Peter Rose, Tomaz Salamun, Craig Sherborne, James Tate, Chris Wallace-Crabbe, Jason Whitmarsh, Dara Wier, Matthew Zapruder, and Andrew Zawacki.

This book is dedicated to my mother.

Publication of this book is supported by a grant from the Pennsylvania Council on the Arts.

Library of Congress Control Number 00-111575
ISBN 0-88748-357-7 Pbk.

10 9 8 7 6 5 4 3 2 1

Contents

III. Diviner

"Yes, few creatures were more natural than I."

ALBERT CAMUS, *The Fall*

Did you find him at the edge of the clearing?

I found him at the edge of the forest.

Did you find him between sleep and sleep?

I found him between the forest and the clearing.

Did you find him lacking clothing?

Did you possess his spirit when you came upon him?

I accepted what he offered freely.

Did he thank you for the deliverance?

Compose a song of gratitude?

He was ardent in his response.

Did the thrush contest your departure?

Did the gauze remain on his eyes?

I could not hear anything for the foliage.

I carry the gauze between sleep and sleep.

I.

Doppelgänger

Insomnia

—and some say it's like the calm after the storm.
Whereas others insist on the morality of the thing.
There are those who will tell you it's the cat's fault, or the fire
  station's.
And those who believe it's a motor inn on wheels that travels
  faster than the speed of light.
A famous mathematician wants to solve its matrix, but must
  approximate due to the lack of concrete boundaries.
Nine people are writing the definitive book on it.
Some college student, thinking it a highball, orders a shot of it.
Fortune tellers everywhere rely on it for advice.
Three dogs—all Doberman pinschers—share its name, as does
  one young girl, from Omaha.
A kid forgot what it was until it came to him bared and gleaming.
He remembered it then—he hasn't known anything else since—

Jasmine Tea

So, too, the woman asleep
on the flea-hopping carpet, golden
Mingo licking her cheek.

To find oneself
at 8:30 in the morning, on a sofa,

a loveseat really, zipper down,
one boot on, eyes
caught, bile on the chin.

Sway to the kitchen,
find life in the cupboards.

No use trying to remember—
nothing to do
but strain upwards.

The house unknown,
and for a moment, even the city.

My Pine Cone Ways

The cicada hum, the crack and splinter
of words from well-wishers, condolence-
givers. The high-five on a Friday afternoon.
"These are the rooms we inhabit,
the corners we have kissed ourselves into."
Love comes in the mornings, lingers
until lunch: bagel, lox and onion
for you, almond waffles with Freestone peaches for me.
"These acts of communion leave us bereft,
so to speak, mute and awkward,
all thumbs when dexterity is essential."
Rooms of varying sizes—
oval the most sensuous, of course,
then dodecahedral, triangular, octagonal
(in that order). The curves of plaster
are forever underrated in the roles they play.
The landlord confiscates the porch swing,
our security deposit dwindles into the red.
We line the kitchen floor with sod,
wait for the roots to dig in.
"Don't you see, these rooms of degrees unknown
feed into each other, occupy all our time,
our thoughts, pineal as they are."
"Don't include me in your pine cone ways."
A pellucid screen at the front door
waylays intruders, the blue light on the ceiling
a sure sign of privacy foretold.
We know we're safe in this stronghold.
The leaves sear into fresh soil,
print our faces in the ground.
The picnic has begun.
We stumble over the influx of pollen.
Swollen membranes will be our death,
the white-faced hornets in the shed our life.

Forecasting at Stonewall Cafe

When I said *clear skies* I found slashed tires.
The Hailstorm of the Century
did not break a single window.

I cannot bring myself to speak
of the tsunami incident.
These unknown, unknowable phenomena . . .

When I get the urge to shout *deluge!*
I yell *jugs!* instead. Skin flakes from my forearms.
"You are an aberration," I tell my neighbor.

I try to fall asleep in the bathroom.
The floors of bars are not known for their comfort
so I call myself wise for postponing the nap.

The family reunion in the back room
is a somber affair: it's a good thing
the architects are tearing the place up.

The waitress has been giving disconcerting looks
all night, but disconcerts no one.
My tonic water went flat hours before.

One eye on the double door, the other
on who slips through its wanton frame,
I keep my glass covered, ready for anything.

Coefficient of Restitution

An elastic collision transferred the energy quite successfully
considering the primitive nature of the equipment and the poor
    lighting
(the electrician quit halfway through the job, never asked for
    anything).
Perhaps you would like to see our new lab, down the hall a bit,

considering the primitive nature of the equipment and the poor
    lighting?
We have applied for several grants from various agencies—
perhaps you would like to see our new lab, down the hall a bit,
where bodies striking against each other can be seen more clearly.

We have applied for several grants from various agencies,
but these things take time, a fact scientists know and must live with.
Where bodies striking against each other can be seen more clearly:
a place we all seek in our final days in the industry.

But these things take time, a fact people know and must live with.
The electrician quit halfway through the job, never asked for
    anything!
The place we all seek in our final days in the industry—
an elastic collision transferred the energy quite successfully.

Garage Sale

They all came by today.
Passersby, browsers, neck-craners.
Big Wheel riders, circus goers. Small time hustlers,
phone tappers, check bouncers, rear enders.
Tattle talers, crank callers, nose pickers.
Water bearers, moped wreckers, trash compactors,
furniture refinishers. Stroller pushers, leaf rakers,
windshield wipers, trash talkers, diaper changers.
Backstabbers, manure shovelers, gem inspectors,
toy breakers. Left-turn-on-red takers.
Baby killers, fortune tellers, right wingers,
bumper stickerers. Neck wringers, forgotten drifters.
Seat belt fasteners, shape shifters. Dizzy spinners,
plain clothes snoopers, house sitters, baby sitters,
couch sitters. They came by. Reckless drivers,
ancient mariners, natural fooders, kindergarten teachers.
Lounge singers, artificial colorers, dog trainers,
spaghetti strainers. Marriage counselors, bargain shoppers.
Lottery losers, hair receders, hair croppers.
Loot stashers, wave riders, wishbone breakers,
wish makers. Drink downers, bet takers,
fat watchers, purse snatchers. Pork barrelers,
farewellers, racetrack gawkers, foreskin snippers.
Butt pinchers, crotch grabbers. They all came by.
Door knockers, shot blockers, mailbox bashers,
fulsome praisers. Nostalgia waxers, coke snorters,
streetwalkers, penny pinchers, orgasm fakers.
Movers and shakers. Cussers, chain smokers,
court jesters. Paddy wagon passengers.
Raggedy Ann clutchers. Belly button pokers,
pipe dreamers. Car bombers, cat nappers,
gun toters, bong hitters. Sword wielders,
sword swallowers, dirty dancers, last chancers.
Dixie whistlers, middle finger givers. Allegiance pledgers,

carpet deodorizers, crap shooters, paper shredders.
Natural selectors, conversation makers. Bread bakers,
contagious yawners, butt kissers, baby kissers,
tree huggers, tree climbers. All of them,
they all came by: so much paint flaking from these walls.

Doppelgänger

I was taught to be the nonexpressive type
but remaining in the shadow of you
on all but the most trivial of occasions
has led me to this, My Final Statement:

What you take to be cat hair
sawdust falling from the ceiling
the sound of air tumbling behind you
I'm taking it with me
The blue ribbon for the 3-legged race
every reptilian belt in the closet
the letter opener from Toledo (Spain)
the Underwood
Most emblems of intellectual exertion
from the spice rack to the spreadsheets
all the love letters in between

Not

. . . and the bloodroot will not grow
where I have stripped the ground of buds—
no *red garment*, no *hellfire*
clings to the body—shirt ruffled
with flame—nor black attire,
which raises *an idea*
of the devil if not the devil
himself.
　　　　　　I present myself
in the color of corn, color of river.
I divest myself of dazzle
—no gold to adorn, no silver,
no paint nor perfumes—
for she who wears these will simmer
and I will pray for her. I will pray
for Loveless Savidge, who spits at the pulpit.
For my sister, yet to be immersed.
For my father, who has assigned himself
to a pit of flame. For my mother.
For the boy who collapsed last Sunday,
his eyes albescent in the rapture
before the flicker.
I must resign myself
not to look upon those eyes again.

Skin

Never mind the fantasy about the tweezers and the tongue,
the one about the bicycle pump and the twisted rim.
Never mind the angle of penetration, or the number
of blessed repetitions in the series of withdrawals and givings-in.

Never mind the dream about the bean-bag chair and the virgin,
the one about the tree and the bull terrier off its chain.
Never mind the song the words will not attach to,
the visions that arrive with the noises next door,

when a sneeze, or a sob, is mistaken for something else
and someone finds himself clinging to the wall,
perhaps with a glass to his ear, or his glasses on,
hoping something dark and old-fashioned has pulled him

from sleep this close to dawn. Never mind the crack
between the blinds and the sill, where a single moan
will keep him waiting an hour for another, his face pressed
against the pane, one eye open, half-blind but guided.

And never mind the woman in the grass beneath the statue.
Her palms are cupping her head, her skirt an inch off-center,
glasses gleaming as the sun hums on the monument
of the general, the skin of her arms slowly going red.

The Investigator Speaks of the Investigation

Everyone in the room confessed
to the cat's drowning.
Z claimed feline phobia, J professed

self-defense, S—frowning—
asserted that it was revenge,
D said the meow-meowing

put her over the edge.
An investigator's nightmare.
Makes one nostalgic for the days of the syringe

and the serum. *Do you swear . . .*

*

I found the cat in the toilet,
clawless, eyes looking nowhere

but downpipe. Now this game of roulette,
spinning the barrel to find the guilty party.
Wipe each finger with a towelette,

dry it, ink it, print it.
A conspiracy, this.

*

To find the truth, to part it

from the lies.
To watch for the will to give,
more or less.

For the constrictive
pupil, for the involuntary blink
or twitch.

For the alibi to sink
and fall
asunder. Outflanked,

they will fidget and jingle
the change in their pockets,
flicker like the flame of a candle.

Tempers will flare. *Fuck its*
and *Fuck yous* will cluster,
eyes like marbles, like rockets.

I will finger the skeletal structure
of their tales, however laconic.
Will lean until they fracture.

Will charge past the rhetoric
to the kernel, the center.
The static will be electric.

And when they're nearly broken, I'll be like a father
to them and threaten their mothers.
I'll turn each against the other—

sister against sister, sister against brother.

Lunar Calendar

A name as simple as Suez
brands itself in your memory,
cat-like in its capacity for flux.

Determined to stay home, you withdraw,
effable as ever, a regular Turgenev.
Forgotten pen pals reassert themselves, this time in Urdu.

Garishly pale, you tilt
however subtly to the south, bypass
instructions handed down for generations, the lunar calendar

just an excuse to avoid a stopover in Iraq,
Kasbah or no Kasbah.
                        "One Alp
loves its brothers" our family credo,
marked in green with that O'Malley sheen.

Nothing but snapshots will keep you warm.
Or, to put it another way, you'll caterwaul,
poltroon that you are, without us at your back.

Quadrilles during our guided hadj,
rock-paper-scissors with swans of origami,
slipping down scree to a collective *Hallelujah!*,
traipsing among cacti and scorpions: that's vacationing!

Under duress, are you? In a huff?
Varicose veins in your mother's calves brought you here—
why spoil her holiday, and to what end?

X. is beautiful this time of year, the natives speak langue d'oc,
you'll adore the tide in its inability to ebb.
Zeus never had it so good. And neither did Leda.

Discovery

Of course no one sets out to discover
artificial insemination, natural selection, wooden dentures
while removing the garbage or paying the cleaner
or adhering to the missionary like an upright quaker:
no one is adequately prepared for the sight of the unfamiliar
for the unfamiliar sight precludes preparation (not to over-
emphasize vision's importance, being the faultiest of our
senses, open to trickery at every global corner:
instances of vision's failures dwell everywhere,
as do instances of failures caused by those failures—
the veteran vacationer who neglects to remember
that abandoning one's spot is always a risky venture
(why someone recommended in some handbook or other
to slip some kid a fiver to sit by the meter
and say he's waiting for his father)—
others' fortunes have been made while some of us rehearse:
cases have been settled, fines levied, and the town's coffers
topped off while we earnest myopians squint into the future,
on the verge of deciding to settle a colony or further
wander, unable to see beyond the third row in the theater,
if the woman on the screen is laughing or dry-heaving: how
     much richer
our home movies and moving patterns would be if we relied on
     another
to show us to our seats—if we let the tongue be our usher).

Roam

To traverse the barren plain our goal,
the notion of common accomplishment
    wanes in porchlight.
Our quadriceps ache and relief
is nowhere if not behind the shoji.
    Your war cry—
"Onward megacephalics!"—
gets you past the gatekeeper
    and into your lean-to.
"Just because" doesn't slip me
into the inner sanctum.
    Our aperçus
weigh heavy on us today.
We forget the lowest denominator
    and its daring escape
into the populace—no escape
at all, just a numb feeling,
    not unlike the slink
and slither of the insincere who rally
the forces for an unforeseen event.
    "This is exactly
what many people do" your lament,
it brings the delivery boy
    to his knees, wallet
proffered for the honor of such wisdom
from one so lens-poppingly
    lordotic, swimmingly
convex (like an eyeball) and concave
(like its socket). "The passage was difficult
    but Lazarus arose on time."

Discretionary Income

Trying to find the center of it all,
the everything heaped up for public delight,
the Post-It that fell behind your desk

with the recipe for happiness,
you announce your decision to pursue
a new course, something neither simple nor expensive,

like the forest green shower curtain
that battles with the puce fiberglass
of the tub, or the electric can opener

with the built-in knife sharpener
that has yet to sharpen its first knife
but is ready for any intruder with a dull one.

You recall numerous precedents for such a decision.
J went to Amsterdam to live for the summer
selling rock and hash, Z left investments to wash dishes,

U bought a cat and named it Elsie-
short-for-Elsinore, C started a band and called it
The Wallace Stevens because her fiancé made her.

People doing things neither simple nor expensive,
except for P, who gave up a charmed life
for a debauched one, and can be found in the bathroom

counting to ten and again, raising not hell,
but the stakes, until there are no takers left
to wager against him.

It's Not the Texture

                              but the consistency
that determines commercial success.
But who's to say what success hangs its hat on?

After all, you should be in friendly waters by now
but are foundering in the family lily pond,
the object of ridicule of more than one stray dog.

The television is nowhere in sight, and the children
are burning leaves, or evidence from a recent crime spree.

The hit man's occupied and so by definition
cannot be a vagabond: it's the unemployed
who find the time to string a series of crimes into a spree.

Tempted to make a metaphor of this sargasso,
you drop the oar: the moon will not fit into an image.

Only the beautiful can be reckless in love,
the rest content to plod a course plotted long ago,
where success is determined by the charts.

The pond's ripples accommodate the stars,
which seem spastic, or at least fitful,
because they're often considered beautiful.

Of course, pain is a condition and all conditions
are temporary, whether or not the weather plays along
and slides those stars into view.

Argonaut Sonata

With no one to stop my launch into panegyric,
I take the warp and weft
in my hands with plans to commandeer this vessel
to a new hemisphere.

Of course, the vessel being sea-wracked
and my atlas bereft
of any destination but the Wessel
Is., I'm sure to founder,

founder of nothing but one phonetic
and the occasional tuft,
tassel
or shock of hair

—cowlicked, no doubt—left
under a trestle, caught unaware.

*

Under a trestle, caught unaware, the vessel
—let's not call the raft
the raft—waxes poetic.
It goes nowhere.

Going nowhere fast, I part and parcel
my belongings onto the craft:
a nonpareil of patchwork.
I perch upon the chair

fastened like the watch to a castle,
wait to be upped and offed,
delivered—anorectic
without the *mal de mer*

or muscles sore from too much work—in swift
and dramatic fashion to Angleterre.

*

No: in frenetic fashion to the Gulf of Carpentaria. And quick.
A true wayfarer,
I see a map as a hassle.
Better to be adrift

and considered quixotic
than safe at harbor,
scissile
and scintillant, admiring one's handicraft.

But such journeys, especially the bound-to-be-historic,
must be an adventure.
They require a dismissal
of conventional statecraft,

a reluctance to pack by list or listlessly prepare,
a refusal to practice sensible thrift.

*

Refusing to practice sensible thrift, I nestle
some wine on board, some Camembert—
a bishop in his bishopric,
properly stuffed and starched and cuffed.

All this hustle and bustle,
all this hoopla and fanfare
—by no means narcissistic—
has attracted something of a crowd. Some seem miffed.

Miffed or not, they're muzzled,
mute in the face of such a dare-
devil who—in this vessel with aquatic
aspirations—sits, stern and abaft.

And the whistle—prepared for this affair,
its blast electric—sends me aloft—

II.

Bystander

1: Notes for a Sequence

To test the silence because it's there to be entered
To suggest to the hawk that its wings are too large
To carve the sand into a semblance of submission
To trail the sound of one disinterred
To construct a voice to withstand the surge
To forego the act to forget the admission
To skew the portrait so carefully centered
To pull the nail to foil the dirge
To permit the request for permission
You scale the notes of the silence that happens
To find a port that might have us

2: Vessel

Because another day brings to light what another day brings,
the anchor gripped for a second then slipped
and nothing of any consequence happened.

Because the motion must be constant,
because the motion subsumes all that comes in contact,
the idea of the ship slides, and, its function forgotten,

the day is no longer a ship but a vessel,
the descent undramatic, slow enough
to go unnoticed by those unacquainted

with the art of the voyage, but this vessel is leaning,
that shore no harbor to hope for.

3: Heart

That fixture
    on which to hang
a capsized vessel,

    the wind nestled
in its ribs, an eel
    picking through the remains

of those who did not survive
    or lift to the surface
to hang there.

4: Abandoned Ship

Nevertheless, the boat is on the rocks.
We conjure all sorts of disasters,
reaching for bloody details of the affair.
A slow forward motion, and then that's it—
this boat leaning on the rocks, rotted through,
its ribs flaked like sponge, the paint chipped, faded.
These rocks have grown used to the weight.
It gives them something to do
besides hug the mud and wait for water.

You say the town should have moved it by now—
rusty nails everywhere luring local kids
into tetanus shots. Maybe it serves
as a warning to would-be drunken sailors,
maybe as a reminder of lives lost,
or livelihoods. Maybe they are waiting
for a concerned neighbor to start something:
hire a truck, sink it, burn it, bury it.
But there is no motion here—the spirit
stagnant, like the water. Like the water.

(Dingle, Ireland)

5: The Old Story

1.

Pond a pool in which to descend
Shunned by water and its sound

Sand assembles a window unpaned
Honed to something less than grind

Found along a shore unmanned
Wind ignores the body of sand

Dares to push against water
Harder than water can bear

2.

That the water laps against the boat
That the water laps against the rocks

That each means something different
To the boat and to the rocks

6: Winter

The river holds down the mud holding up the river.
Nothing stirs, nothing is stirring in the river.
We watch each other, not the oppressive water.
Nothing sings at the river, the only sound the chatter
of flying foxes—they hang to shreds in the trees, shatter
foliage.
                Yesterday it was summer; today, winter.
In an hour the sun will turn air to swelter.
In an hour the wind will rake this shelter.

The only birds black swans—they will charge
for food. They thrive on your fear.
Nor will they sing. Their noise won't damage the air,
the sound of our listening.
                We listen, but who will hear
the sound of our listening? Not that girl over there,
crawling among the reeds.
                Broken. Breathless. Large.

(South Melbourne, Australia)

7: Epithalamium

The haar refuses to approach this coast,
to bring its glossolalia of fish to the shore.
The glottal stops of waves on rocks
recall another tongue.
                    The detour
written in the clouds has brought us
to this harbor—no haven from the stars' dull ache.
They seem ready to break from the augered slab
balanced above us. Somehow they adhere.

Someone is singing, *the ties that bind*
the only words to arrive. They unravel at our feet,
take their place in the inscription of sea wrack
as you shoulder the wind and its revenants
and I wait for the strands of a new morning
to lurch over the other edge, incarnadine, and defeat
what stands before it. Yet that song is flowing
and flown, its singer's whereabouts still unknown.

(St. Andrews, Scotland)

8: Iconostasis for Absence

Rope against wood is another sound.
It places you on your bike at the clay hills,
where the syntax of absence is a coin
slipped from under the tongue. A rope
rocks on its perch in the oak. It's snapped.
A sjambok when the wind cracks.
Less than its former self, but a rope yet.
You used it for something
but cannot pull the image down.
Of course the hills are gone,
and a line of stores—farrago of need—
fills the gap.
                That red a nimbus.
Bulldozers stripping curves off the land.
You cannot call the land dead, the hills ghosts,
the rope a frayed soul. Absence need not translate
into daemon Grief. It has no referent.

(Short Pump, Virginia)

9: Bystander

Not shamed as a struck branch will quake,
not a match that refuses to flame, the oar
creaks against the boat and smacks the surface
of the lake, neither emerald nor amethyst.
The chorale of wood on water recalls
the clamor before the hood is delivered
and dumped over the bystander's head
by another bystander's blisterless hands.
No song is heard there, no listeners for the taking.

No song is heard here, no listeners for the taking.
Trees reach for bottom-scum farther
than they stretch. Their music breaks no one's heart,
but the boy in the boat, distracted by some call
or hum, lets an oar slip and gather
water as it sinks then rises. Everything must sink
before it can float: the boy makes a note
of it, leans for the oar—having carved
its corona onto the lake—and rows.

(Powhatan, Virginia)

10: Denouement

Swollen tar-smoke rises, a yellow siren pulses,
    mangled steel in tow.

You move from the hood to the driver's seat
    and turn the key.

The digital clock eases on, over an hour gone.
    The line of cars lurches

to attention and gradually scatters. An egret
    circling on the right:

it alights on a shack, the heat breaking the air between.

(Key West-Key Largo, Florida)

11: Prelapsarian

The silence of the banyans blinds.
They strain to understand the little things:
salt wounds, osmosis, the natural order.

He can taste blood when she strolls by
—in his nose, under the tongue of stars—
bones bared to harm, roots scarcely concealed.

They wait to adjust to better days.

12: Self-Portrait in a Late Hour

The summer holds the day to its word.

A solitary heron, orange
in the gleam, seems strange here.

The water shattered, the child,
on this, the last day of summer, holds.

A treasure in every corner,
the house breaks into flesh.

Were it not for the rule against it,
the house would break into song.

They seem to hesitate.
The child is running ahead of them.

The windows hold nothing out. Or in.
Rooms prepare for this arrival.

The wind holds nothing back.
There they are, beneath the archways.

There they are beneath the ruins.

after Yves Bonnefoy

III.

Diviner

Gravity

Before the hole in the yard expands to glacial size,
before the porch eats the house in two,
the house that buries itself beneath the grass
yet rocks with each hard wind,

the tree gives and comes down on a gust,
not the one that sends the porch into the ground,
not the one that pulls water from wood,

and the tree, delivered to the wind at last,
goes through the air with a purposeless grace,
spins along an axis unknown to the slow

as you watch it, having heard it first,
and wonder what it takes to move that fast—
more than lightness, or a frame almost full,
a matter less of weight than of mass.

2.

You tromp among the branches iced and felled
by ice, slide a finger down to grab
and crunch what's frozen until what's frozen falls,
clinks against the grass that snaps against each step.

To see the limbs in gleaming descent, you pull
and shake until you hear the tree tighten
to flash, and look toward the sound of the crash —

a treeful of ice raining swift, the sun
a caul wherever ice is, more intent
in its presence in this aftermath than ice is.

3.

The rough between the hulls
succumbs to lesser views:
horseshoe crabs and stingrays hold

sand between their teeth
                              and grin
or seem to
                    in such light that brings
the human to every empty thing.

Undone from its limbs, your body
is snapped back with each big pulse
to repeat the longing for movement
that has carried it this far
                              and carries it still.

There is a nearness in this dirt. A nearness

The space where you were calms down: everything is veiled: horses
stamp the soil, entire orchards ripening

Everything veiled, you wait for firmness beneath your feet: entire
orchards ripening, a rhythmic cracking

Waiting for firmness beneath it, the fattened wind prowls in the
branches: a rhythmic cracking brings you a false sense of
achievement

The fattened wind prowling in the branches, the scent of hay
brings you a sense of false achievement: you choke on future glory

The scent of hay: stridency gives way to softness choking on future
glory: the smell of must settles

Stridency giving way to softness, the sound of horses stamping soil,
the smell of must settles on you: the space where you were calms
down

after Edvard Kocbek

Frame

The window rushes
against the hill's empty sleeve.

Walls brown and fat
through the frame,

grief poses in a dress
pushed between the sisters.

The hill raps its sharp stones
on the house's broken collar—

residue of tar and slag,
curtain on a branch.

A finch perches
on a clutch of sticks.

*

The shock of smoke
threaded through sockets:

the crack of iron and pine,
box spring and mattress:

an acoustics of sinews—
ball and joint,

shard and cataract,
corona on the retina.

Flames and flames
wake the shut doors.

Whine and whirr
under the skirt.

Wings blur
and repeat

in the clutter,
between sheaves of light.

*

Free of leather
the horse leans

into a sun
that grinds

the hill into something
like scorched grass.

Churn and spin:
the flames in the house

on the hill
ridden with medlar.

A strip of linen
snaps once and goes.

Coign of Vantage

1.

A horse and a mule stand head to tail in a pasture.
The horse's tail swings at the flies around the mule's face.
The grass, blanched and brittle, has been chewed to the roots
where the horse and the mule stand, tail to head.
A pond green with algae on the other side
of the road, rutted, impassable. A girl follows
a sheepdog to the pond. She plans to catch something.
Even the horse and the mule know better.

2.

The horse is a hoodlum,
the mule his hanger-on,
the pasture an alley.
The horse pulls the knife
from his pocket, his lips
a shutter for the disaster
that's his mouth, in the shadow
the mule casts as it hovers.
There is no dog.
The mule ignores
the flies at his face,
watches the horse watch
the girl. The girl is a girl
hoping to get home. Even
the horse and the mule know better.

Shelter

Full-tilt and on kilter, the swelter
    of daggers swathes byways through fields
    of diggers and sweepers, payment for pardons
fallen by broadsides and shells.

They fray disgrace into hills: the blaze
    in tessellated chords wracks convictions
    into second songs, second thoughts into finales
that fry to nothing before they flare:

rust gathers its fellows into ranks of behave,
    weeds wrench through pinion and the rack
    words stretch themselves across as cries
roost in the shelter of scree, on command.

The demand of sleep scratches its initials,
the damned lean—they lean into sleep's wager.

Looking Back on It

The decision to bomb the outskirts of the town,
the wish to bring the mission (and the war)
to completion, the nights filled with fire, the days of sleep,
a casual conversation with more-
than-casual results, the nothing happening,
the silkworm threading its life, the eyes stung with sweat,
the near-escape, then the next, the falling off,
the pursuit in air, the pursuit on foot,
a lucky break, the conduit discovered,
flesh on flesh on fire on the roof,
the razor blade, the exotic everything,
the impossible distance breached at last,
natural light curling, bat guano building,
a run for cover and a dive into bushes,
the cut behind the ear, the sand between the toes,
the flexibility of schedule, the imposition
turned us in a certain direction
that, once we were on course, kept us going,
not sustaining us, but not destroying us,
not yet, and the curve of it all, the trajectory
captured for us the moment,
not transcendent, not epiphanic,
but not earthly either, and clear vision
was the last thing we wanted, could endure.

Diviner

Fracture my brother, in the form of wither
   I steer toward the city no frost will abide.
Structure my winter, holster my rumble,
   I bear these reins of slumbrous design.
Passage to prescience garnered at dawn,
   the troops acknowledge the friction of thrall,
presage of pretense clambering skyward.
   The traps scorched and stubbled—such weather
no water can assuage the strain of—
   I trace paths of dim presence
no mortar can crack, and, tilting windward,
   I slice into the curve then crash the return
from keeper to keepsake, the way forward
from station to stalemate only a diviner can navigate.

Something Given to Make Whole Among the Ruses

that are shattered by the large
derailments no plot has sprung
untoward guilt by dissociation
the clatter in the hallway calls
attention to the demolition
at Flinders & Swanston the office
emptied by premonition and the lunch rush
the hair stylist's clippers driving
the newly shorn to distraction
the physics of attraction and reduction
constructions no more of pencils and slide rules
oh where has the abacus left us
no explosion will take place here
folks sorry for your rubble
The Trouble With Spectacle
in Three Thousand Words or Less
guidelines available in Appendix B
which city doesn't have its history
of falling buildings rats going down
between walls a rodenticide
on sky-scraping levels
the roaches will shake off the drop and dust
and be in someone's kitchen by dusk
whose hands break at the sound
of something breaking and who's in charge
of the still parade the prayer meeting
across the bridge a protest against sacrilege
whose hammer will shatter the image
of our son immersed who has his finger
on the switch to bring each high rise down

Self-Portrait

Not as fire wrapped in a barrel
Not the snap of wood at the horizon line
The ash-heap swiveling
The cistern at the wall
Not a step through gimcrack or quoin
Locus of melt and plinth, rib and splinter
Not the laying of stone on blood-mortared stone
Not a hand hewn for the task
Not a voice resting in the crease
In the leaves that swirl and turn, swirl and turn
Pivot before they lift, and catch
Not a thing held as the candle at that cradle
Not a match not a match not a match

Waver

Fragments of bone constellate
                              cross-field, drawn through dirt
to split and rear asunder
—frigate wrapped in foam, spar shaken to scrap—

to splice the column (of boys) wielding/unwielding
implements sharp or explosive,
to splay, to rip them from their encasements (of flesh)

—implying the will to decide such an act—
through chorales lines of impact waver
—empiricists of death—
                              before the strike that wrecks light

through cane-brake and lens—quotient and integral—
intervals of nod and stagger,
through columns of columns no shekinah

intervenes for: the pallor of smoke from stacks
intervolves the limbs that crack, and crack.

Veterans' Club

Those who ignore the news from that country are drinking with
    those who exercise themselves
with every fact of every death, every figure, image, and quote that
    tallies or tells
who deserves rebuke—*the world is full of voices*—and who some
    help: cans, clothes, and prayers
for the ones under siege in that maimed town. Those who ignore
    the pain the news portrays,

the pain it portends—*some are lulled, then hurled by each*—lean
    into the half-light
stripping the bar of its veneer, their glasses diminishing by the hour
    their focus on the screen, half-lit
while "Harvest Moon" recycles itself on the jukebox, skipping at
    the third refrain, then going
across the record's scratch (the boy on a run at the table needs the
    song for the balls to go in).

With last call at ten to two, with the boy's grin due to expire, those
    who ignore
and those more aware make sure both hands are full against
    friction and the hand of war.

The box is unplugged mid-song, the 8 knocked into the night's last
    pocket, the cues returned
to the rack: those who ignore and those more aware unsettle
    themselves from their stools, having learned

a score, or two, who fucked whom the night before, or got fucked,
    and head together for the door,
where their cars wait to take them—*in solemn troops and sweet
    society*—home to their private war.

Extremities

This instance of weather exudes elements of chance uncommon
In lacks such as this, the power of persuasion less power than curse:

Sleep skirmished, like-minded principles applied else discarded,
The knack for precision locates its least predictable hell as mayhem

Is ushered into the gap being bridged as we speak, yet we say we
    know
How calmness ceases to be a matter of will, and continue

In our insistence upon all that foresees what balance rejects as
    crooked
Posture: light freighting itself across the country by surface and
    surfeit,

Mile by mile until it arrives in tattered splendor well after
You stopped expecting it, the carrier's regrets stitched into the
    missive

No longer massive or proper but massively popular: junk weighs less
Than its weight in gold, the carrier says, throwing his self onto his
    other,

An act no caster of weather foretold.

Ghazal

Quarter in hand to see "Raising the Dead,"
but they forget everything, the dead.

The Flood of '94 in Georgia?
Flint River pulled coffins, spinning the dead.

Formaldehyde, forceps and scalpel . . .
we spend the weekend examining the dead.

My father, a betting man, lost it all:
"The only sure thing? . . . The dead."

You run your fingers through my hair,
combing the healthy and clipping the dead.

You and the rest of your sleep—
why this matter of visiting the dead?

My fiancée the parlor beautician:
she's so radiant rouging the dead!

I promised myself many weapons
for prodding and impaling the dead.

Know what my Uncle Clovis said?
"I heard them laughing, the dead."

And of course, that banker on the ledge:
"They don't worry about a thing, the dead!"

Now count them, touch them all!
But they get nothing, the dead.

What They Remember

For the record he assiduously adhered to the speed limit
Except for that one time
That time he daisied around the bend
They say he pursued the lascivious side of life until the end
He fell in with the religious crowd while an infant
That squirrel still carries a pellet behind the ear
They say he was a generous man
Orphanages foreclosed in his name
He always knocked before entering
They say he had a tendency to enter through a bathroom window
And no one home
And no one home
They say he never broke a bone
He never spliced a comma
Or used exclamation points in a profligate manner
The Fourth of July was his favorite holiday
The fireworks scared him half to death
They say the Fates smiled on him at birth
Someone cut the cord
He'd no sooner look you in the eye than salute the president
They say his car would stop on a dime
They say he drove an injured animal to church on Sundays
And put his groceries in the trunk
They say the groceries sat in the front

With that poor animal in the trunk

They say he had a nervous twitch

He never owned a bird

They say he drove his cockatoo crazy with his continual knitting

He wove his way into highfalutin circles

He didn't know a thing about antiques

They say a peeping Tom at the window caught his eye

The rest of him remained free

Freedom of choice kept him awake

He slept only on Wednesday

He slept like the dead on vacation in Cuba

They say he could play any tune by ear

A keen financial acumen marked his life

They say he bled the coffers dry

He paid his tithes religiously

Any sudden movement would throw him completely off kilter

He looked cute in a skirt

They say he could thread a needle with his eyes closed

He peeked when in public

They say he never missed a beat

You couldn't knock it out of him

They say he could have been in the movies

He forgot a line or two at times

He recovered remarkably well for his age

They say he had a thing for candles

Brittle brittle days

They say he shot the bolt a bit early now and then
Now and then he stayed in for the long haul
He got caught with his pants down once
Under the bleachers
Under a full moon in the park
They say he never bounced a check
For honor is all a man has
What good is a man without honor
He yelled Damn! when he fell from the monkey bars
For honor is all a man has
He forged solid relations with his neighbors
They say he could hit a nail on the head
They say he never worried about mutual funds
Compound interest drove him to the brink
He never touched the stuff
Except on Wednesday
He pitched horseshoes on Wednesdays
On Wednesday he was puritanical about everything
His ancestors were tramontanes
Hard to pin down
You couldn't pin down his ancestors
For they were tramontanes
They say his soul outshone the sun
They say we didn't know him as well as they did
He made no mention of that squirrel in his will
They say he didn't give anyone anything

Notes

"Not": Christine Leigh Heyrman, *Southern Cross: The Beginnings of the Bible Belt.*

"Skin": Monument Avenue, Richmond, Virginia.

"The Old Story" (part 2): Frank Kuppner, *Ridiculous! Absurd! Disgusting!*

"Iconostasis for Absence" is for Andrew Zawacki.

"Frame": Odysseus Elytis, "Clepsydras of the Unknown."

The title and first line of "Something Given to Make Whole Among the Ruses" are from Wallace Stevens' "From the Journal of Crispin." The poem also alludes to the controversy—protests and threats—surrounding the Andres Serrano exhibit at the National Gallery of Victoria in Melbourne, Australia, in 1997.

"Self-Portrait": Cormac McCarthy, *The Stonemason.*

"Veterans' Club": Henry Vaughan, "Distraction"; Shakespeare, *King Richard the Second*; Milton, "Lycidas."

"Ghazal": Paul Celan, *Breathturn* (Pierre Joris' translation).

Biographical Information

Born in Columbus, Ohio in 1972, Brian Henry was raised in Virginia and educated at the College of William and Mary and at the University of Massachusetts at Amherst. He lived in Australia from 1997 to 1998 on a Fulbright grant and was poetry editor of *Meanjin* that year. *Astronaut* first appeared in England in 2000 from Arc Publications and was later shortlisted for the Forward Prize. *Astronaut* was also published in Slovenia in translation by Mondena Publishing in 2000. Henry's poems have appeared in numerous magazines around the world, including *American Poetry Review, The New Republic, The Paris Review, New American Writing, TriQuarterly, Stand,* and *Jacket.* He reviews poetry for the *Times Literary Supplement, The Kenyon Review,* and *Boston Review,* among other places. He edits *Verse* and Verse Press, and teaches at the University of Georgia in Athens.

Recent Titles in the Carnegie Mellon Poetry Series

1998
Yesterday Had a Man In It, Leslie Adrienne Miller
Definition of the Soul, John Skoyles
Dithyrambs, Richard Katrovas
Postal Routes, Elizabeth Kirschner
The Blue Salvages, Wayne Dodd
The Joy Addict, James Harms
Clemency and Other Poems, Colette Inez
Scattering the Ashes, Jeff Friedman
Sacred Conversations, Peter Cooley
Life Among the Trolls, Maura Stanton

1999
Justice, Caroline Finkelstein
Edge of House, Dzvinia Orlowsky
A Thousand Friends of Rain:
New and Selected Poems, 1976-1998, Kim Stafford
The Devil's Child, Fleda Brown Jackson
World as Dictionary, Jesse Lee Kercheval
Vereda Tropical, Ricardo Pau-Llosa
The Museum of the Revolution, Angela Ball
Our Master Plan, Dara Wier

2000
Small Boat with Oars of Different Size, Thom Ward
Post Meridian, Mary Ruefle
The Hierarchies of Rue, Roger Sauls
Constant Longing, Dennis Sampson
Mortal Education, Joyce Peseroff
How Things Are, James Richardson
Years Later, Gregory Djanikian
On the Waterbed They Sank to Their Own Levels,
        Sarah Rosenblatt

Blue Jesus, Jim Daniels
Winter Morning Walks; 100 Postcards to Jim Harrison,
    Ted Kooser

2001
The Deepest Part of the River, Mekeel McBride
The Origin of Green, T. Alan Broughton
Day Moon, Jon Anderson
Glacier Wine, Maura Stanton
Earthly, Michael McFee
Lovers in the Used World, Gillian Conoley
Ten Thousand Good Mornings, James Reiss
The World's Last Night, Margot Schilpp
Mastodon, 80% Complete, Jonathan Johnson
The Sex Lives of the Poor and Obscure, David Schloss
Voyages in English, Dara Wier
Quarters, James Harms

2002
Astronaut, Brian Henry
Among the Musk Ox People, Mary Ruefle
The Finger Bone, Kevin Prufer
Keeping Time, Suzanne Cleary
From the Book of Changes, Stephen Tapscott
What It Wasn't, Laura Kasischke
The Late World, Arthur Smith
Slow Risen Among the Smoke Trees, Elizbeth Kirschner